# ROCK EXPLORER

# MINERALS

## Claudia Martin

Quarto is the authority on a wide range of topics.

Quarto educates, entertains and enriches the lives of our readers—enthusiasts and lovers of hands-on living.

www.quartoknows.com

Editor: Clare Hibbert
Designer: Dave Ball

First Published in 2017 by QED Publishing,
an imprint of The Quarto Group.
The Old Brewery, 6 Blundell Street,
London N7 9BH, United Kingdom.
T (0)20 7700 6700 F (0)20 7700 8066
www.QuartoKnows.com

A catalogue record for this book is available from the British Library.

ISBN 978-1-78493-964-9

Manufactured in Guangdong, China TT022018

9 8 7 6 5 4 3 2 1

MIX
Paper from
responsible sources
FSC® C016973

# Contents

# What is a Mineral?

Minerals are solids that grow in the ground or in water. There are around 5,000 different minerals.

## BUILDING BLOCKS

Minerals are made of pure, simple substances called elements. There are more than 100 elements. Everything on Earth is made up of elements.

▲ This mineral, quartz, is made from the elements silicon and oxygen.

## MINERAL MIX

Some minerals grow when different elements join together. Others contain just one element.

▼ Rhodocrosite is a mineral made from the elements carbon, oxygen and manganese.

### Rocky mix-up

Rocks are mixtures of minerals. The main mineral in the rock quartzite is quartz, but there are others too.

◄ Diamond is a mineral made from only one element: carbon.

# How Minerals
# Grow

Minerals grow when the tiniest parts of an element, called atoms, stick to other atoms.

## GROWING UNDERGROUND

Beneath the Earth's surface is hot, runny rock called magma. When the magma cools, atoms start to stick together.

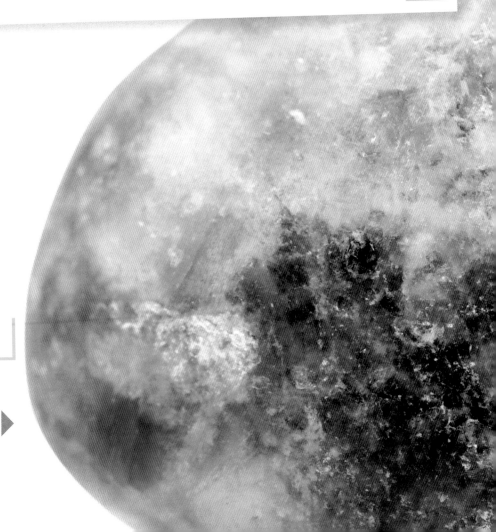

Lepidolite grows in cooling magma. It is made from atoms of silicon, oxygen, potassium and other elements.

# GROWING IN WATER

Water often has atoms of different elements in it. When water evaporates (floats away as a gas), those atoms are left behind.

Gypsum grows when water evaporates and leaves behind calcium and sulphur.

## Rare or not?

Common minerals such as quartz are made from elements that are common in rocks or water. Other minerals, such as brookite, are very rare.

This brookite crystal formed in quartz.

# Amazing
# **Crystals**

If a mineral has plenty of room, it grows in a regular shape called a crystal.

Epidote crystals form tall, slanted rectangles.

## REPEATING PATTERN

When a mineral starts to form, its atoms stick to each other in a special pattern. If nothing interrupts the growing mineral, it carries on building the same pattern.

Scolecite often grows as groups of thin needles.

# SIGNATURE SHAPE

You can identify minerals by the shape of their crystals.

Vanadinite crystals form six-sided shapes called hexagons.

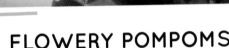

▲ Pyrite crystals can form cubes.

## FLOWERY POMPOMS

In damp caves, aragonite crystals can make flower-like shapes. They form when dripping water contains calcium and carbon.

▲ Amazonite crystals grow into wedge shapes.

# Bright and
# **Beautiful**

Some minerals have strong colours.
Different elements make different colours.

## MULTICOLOURED MINERAL

Elbaite comes in every colour of the rainbow. One crystal can be more than one colour.

Red and green elbaite crystals are called 'watermelon'.

# GORGEOUS GEMS

Some beautifully coloured, hard minerals are used to decorate jewellery. They are known as gemstones.

Aquamarine is a beryl crystal, made sea-blue by traces of iron.

A ruby is a crystal of the mineral corundum, tinted red by the element chromium.

## Paint palette

*In the past, some minerals were ground to make colourful paint. Azurite made a deep blue.*

**Powdered azurite**

Citrine is a quartz crystal, yellowed with a little iron.

# Shining **Metals**

Metals are found in rocks. They are minerals too! Pure metals contain just one element.

### METALLIC FEATURES

Metals are shiny, strong and melt when heated. They are used to make jewellery, coins and machinery.

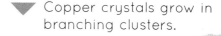

These gold crystals formed on a piece of quartz.

Copper crystals grow in branching clusters.

## Most expensive

*The metal rhodium is far more expensive than gold. It is used in special machines that cut down the pollution given out by cars.*

This machine cuts down car pollution. It contains rhodium. ▶

# AWESOME ORES

Some minerals contain metals mixed with other elements. These minerals are called ores. They are mined and then heated to remove the useful metal.

▲ The mineral magnetite contains the metal iron.

The mineral sphalerite is ▶ an ore of the metal zinc.

# Strange and
# Powerful

Some minerals behave very strangely.
You could say they have super powers!

## GLOWING AND FADING

A few minerals do odd things
when they are exposed to light.
Autunite glows in the dark after
it has soaked up ultraviolet light.

Proustite is red
until it is put in
sunlight. Then
it turns dark.

**Autunite**

# TICK TOCK

If you pass electricity through quartz, it shakes at a regular pace. Many watches contain a tiny quartz crystal, which keeps them ticking evenly.

**Watch battery**

**Quartz crystal is in here.**

▲ A watch's battery sends electricity to a quartz crystal.

**Quartz crystal**

## Giant gypsum

The biggest mineral crystals ever discovered were 11 m long. The gypsum crystals grew in a hot, wet cave in Mexico.

Record-breaking ▶ gypsum crystals

# Most
# **Deadly**

Do not be deceived by the beauty of these minerals. They could be killers!

### CAUTION!
Minerals are poisonous if they contain poisonous elements. Orpiment contains arsenic, which was used to kill rats and insects.

Cinnabar contains poisonous mercury.

**Orpiment**

Stibnite used to be shaped into knives and forks, until people realized it was poisonous.

## KILLER KOHL

The ancient Egyptians used the mineral galena to make dark eyeliner called kohl. Galena contains lead, which can damage the brain if swallowed.

Galena

The Egyptians made eye ▲ make-up with minerals.

## RADIOACTIVE

Minerals that contain the element uranium are radioactive. This means they release energy that can damage human bodies.

◀ This mineral, uranophane, contains radioactive uranium.

# Hunting for
# **Minerals**

Minerals are dug out of the ground by miners. You can also look for them yourself.

## LUCKY BREAK

The best places to hunt for minerals are where rocks are broken open. Running water and waves break open rocks on beaches and riverbeds.

▶ This lucky collector has found quartz.

## MINING

Metals and gemstones are just some of the minerals that are mined from the ground.

▼ These underground workers are mining gold.

### Prehistoric mine

One of the world's oldest mines is in Swaziland, Africa. More than 40,000 years ago, miners there dug up haematite to make red paint.

# Useful
# **Minerals**

There are lots of useful minerals. You can find them in factories, fields, homes and food!

## LOOKING GOOD

The mineral fluorite is used in toothpaste to make teeth white and strong. Mica adds shine to lipsticks and nail varnish.

Fluorite helps to stop tooth decay.

Gleaming mica in a mica mine

## TRULY TASTY

Farmers fertilize their crops with phosphorus, a mineral found in apatite. Food itself is seasoned with salt, a mineral called halite.

Halite is dug from mines or collected from evaporated seawater.

Apatite contains phosphorus, which helps plants grow.

## GETTING CREATIVE

Minerals are used by artists in paints and pencils. Craftworkers such as potters or glassblowers use them too.

Feldspar is used to make glass and pottery.

Pencil 'lead' is not really the metal lead. It is the soft mineral graphite.

# Mineral Guide

### ARAGONITE
**Colour:** Usually white, but may be coloured
**Where to find:** In caves and around hot springs

### AZURITE
**Colour:** Bright blue
**Where to find:** In rocks close to the metal copper

### CINNABAR
**Colour:** Red
**Where to find:** In rocks close to volcanoes

### DIAMOND
**Colour:** Usually colourless
**Where to find:** Deep underground; brought nearer to the surface by moving magma

### EPIDOTE
**Colour:** Usually green
**Where to find:** In rock that has been heated

### GOLD
**Colour:** Golden yellow
**Where to find:** In rocks, often mixed with silver; sometimes in small flakes in streams

### GYPSUM
**Colour:** Usually colourless or pale
**Where to find:** In caves; in limestone and clay

### MAGNETITE
**Colour:** Grey to black
**Where to find:** In rock that has been heated

### PYRITE
**Colour:** Yellow to grey
**Where to find:** In a wide range of rocks

### QUARTZ
**Colour:** Colourless when pure; may be any colour
**Where to find:** Common in many rocks and pebbles

# Glossary

**atom** The smallest parts of an element that can exist by themselves.

**crystal** The regular shape that a mineral forms as it grows.

**element** A pure, basic substance.

**evaporate** Turn from a liquid into a gas.

**gemstone** A beautiful and hard mineral or rock that is used in jewellery.

**magma** Hot, runny rock that lies beneath Earth's surface of cool, hardened rock.

**metal** A solid that is usually hard and shiny. Metal melts when it is heated and can also be hammered into new shapes.

**mineral** A solid formed in the ground or in water. Each mineral is a mix of elements.

**ore** A rock or mineral that contains a useful metal.

**pollution** Damage to the air, water or soil by human actions. Exhaust fumes from cars are a form of air pollution.

**radioactive** Giving off a dangerous form of energy.

**rock** A solid made from different minerals.

**ultraviolet light** Light rays that are beyond the violet end of the spectrum and that cannot be seen by the human eye.

# Index

24

## PICTURE CREDITS